The 75 Day-Gratitude Journal, Mandala Coloring

&

Other Activities
That Will Bring Out The Best in You

The Benefits of Gratitude Journaling

The benefits of Gratitude journaling can be grouped into:
Health Benefits
Career Benefits
Social Benefits
Emotional Benefits
Personality Benefits

Emotional Benefits

- Gratitude journaling will make you happier.
- Gratitude journaling will help in increasing psychological emotions.
- Gratitude journaling will aid your self-esteem.
- Gratitude journaling will not allow thoughts of suicide comes into play.

Social Benefits

- Gratitude journaling will make people like you.
- Gratitude will enhance your social support.
- Gratitude journaling will help your relationship with others.
- Gratitude journaling enhances your romantic relationships.

Personality Benefits

- Gratitude journaling will you to be more optimistic.
- Gratitude journaling will help your spirituality.
- Gratitude journaling will you teach an act of giving more.
- Gratitude journaling reduces the desire for materialism.

Career Benefits

- Gratitude journaling will make you in finding meaning in your work or job.
- Gratitude journaling will aid you in the improvement of work concerning mental health to reduce stress.

Health Benefits

- Gratitude journaling will help you in reducing depressive symptoms.
- Gratitude journaling will enhance deep sleep.
- Gratitude journaling will help you in reducing blood pressure.
- Gratitude journaling will enhance overall physical health.

How to use The 75-Day Gratitude Journal, Mandala Coloring & Other Activities

Steps:

1. Meditate on the quote

2. Write out three things that you are thankful for the day

3. Pick your colored pen and give life to the mandala. As you do this, meditate on what you have subconsciously picked during the day.

4. Write out activities that made you happy that day.

5. Write out your thoughts and ideas for the day.

6. Tick the box to reveal how you feel majorly during the day.

7. Write out your to-do list for the next day.

Day 1

Date_______________

> Three meals plus bedtime make four
> sure blessings a day.
> — Mason Cooley

I'm thankful of....

I'm thankful of....

I'm thankful of....

Give the image life!

Activities that made me happy today...

1.
2.
3.
4.
5.

My thoughts and ideas today.....

What to do Tomorrow?

1 _______________________________
2 _______________________________
3 _______________________________
4 _______________________________
5 _______________________________

How Do I Feel Today?

Tired ☐

Feelings of Love ☐

Crying ☐

Sleepy ☐

Smiling ☐

Winking ☐

Day 2

Date _______________

> If the only prayer you said in your whole life
> was "thank you" that would suffice.
> - Meister Eckhart

I'm thankful of....

I'm thankful of....

I'm thankful of....

Give the image life!

Activities that made me happy today...

1.
2.
3.
4.
5.

My thoughts and ideas today.....

What to do Tomorrow?

1 ________________________
2 ________________________
3 ________________________
4 ________________________
5 ________________________

Tired

Feelings of Love

Crying

Sleepy

Smiling

Winking

Day 3

Date______________

> Gratitude is riches. Complaint is poverty
> - Doris Day

I'm thankful of....

I'm thankful of....

I'm thankful of....

Give the image life!

Activities that made me happy today...

1.
2.
3.
4.
5.

My thoughts and ideas today......

What to do Tomorrow?

1 _______________________
2 _______________________
3 _______________________
4 _______________________
5 _______________________

How Do I Feel Today?

Tired

Feelings of Love

Crying

Sleepy

Smiling

Winking

Day 4

Date _______________

So much has been given to me; I have no time to ponder over that which has been denied.

- Helen Keller

I'm thankful of....

I'm thankful of....

I'm thankful of....

Give the image life!

Activities that made me happy today...

1.
2.
3.
4.
5.

My thoughts and ideas today.....

What to do Tomorrow?

1 __________________________________
2 __________________________________
3 __________________________________
4 __________________________________
5 __________________________________

How Do I Feel Today?

Tired

Feelings of Love

Crying

Sleepy

Smiling

Winking

Day 5

Date____________

> If a fellow isn't thankful for what he's got,
> he isn't likely to be thankful for what he's
> going to get.
>   - Frank A. Clark

I'm thankful of....

I'm thankful of....

I'm thankful of....

Give the image life!

Activities that made me happy today...

1.
2.
3.
4.
5.

My thoughts and ideas today.....

What to do Tomorrow?

1 _______________________
2 _______________________
3 _______________________
4 _______________________
5 _______________________

How Do I Feel Today?

Tired

Feelings of Love

Crying

Sleepy

Smiling

Winking

Day 6

Date______________

> Gratitude is the most exquisite form of courtesy.
> - Jacques Maritain

I'm thankful of....

I'm thankful of....

I'm thankful of....

Give the image life!

Activities that made me happy today...

1.
2.
3.
4.
5.

My thoughts and ideas today.....

What to do Tomorrow?

1 _______________________
2 _______________________
3 _______________________
4 _______________________
5 _______________________

How Do I Feel Today?

Tired

Feelings of Love

Crying

Sleepy

Smiling

Winking

Day 7

Date __________

> *An early morning walk is a blessing for the whole day.*
> - Henry David Thoreau

I'm thankful of....

I'm thankful of....

I'm thankful of....

Give the image life!

Activities that made me happy today...

1.
2.
3.
4.
5.

My thoughts and ideas today.....

What to do Tomorrow?

1 _______________________
2 _______________________
3 _______________________
4 _______________________
5 _______________________

How Do I Feel Today?

Tired

Feelings of Love

Crying

Sleepy

Smiling

Winking

Day 8

Date _______________

> Stop now. Enjoy the moment. It's now or
> never
>
> \- Maxime Lagacé

I'm thankful of....

I'm thankful of....

I'm thankful of....

Give the image life!

Activities that made me happy today...

1.
2.
3.
4.
5.

My thoughts and ideas today.....

What to do Tomorrow?

1 _______________________________
2 _______________________________
3 _______________________________
4 _______________________________
5 _______________________________

How Do I Feel Today?

Tired

Feelings of Love

Crying

Sleepy

Smiling

Winking

Day 9

Date_____________

I'm thankful of....

I'm thankful of....

I'm thankful of....

Give the image life!

Activities that made me happy today...

1.
2.
3.
4.
5.

My thoughts and ideas today.....

What to do Tomorrow?

1 _______________________
2 _______________________
3 _______________________
4 _______________________
5 _______________________

How Do I Feel Today?

Tired

Feelings of Love

Crying

Sleepy

Smiling

Winking

Day 10

Date _______________

I'm thankful of….

I'm thankful of….

I'm thankful of….

Give the image life!

Activities that made me happy today...

1.
2.
3.
4.
5.

My thoughts and ideas today.....

What to do Tomorrow?

1 _______________________
2 _______________________
3 _______________________
4 _______________________
5 _______________________

How Do I Feel Today?

Tired

Feelings of Love

Crying

Sleepy

Smiling

Winking

Day 11

Date_______________

> *In all affairs, it's a healthy thing now and then to hang a question mark on the things you have long taken for granted.*
> - Bertrand Russell

I'm thankful of....

I'm thankful of....

I'm thankful of....

Give the image life!

Activities that made me happy today...

1.
2.
3.
4.
5.

My thoughts and ideas today.....

What to do Tomorrow?

1
2
3
4
5

How Do I Feel Today?

Tired

Feelings of Love

Crying

Sleepy

Smiling

Winking

Day 12

Date______________

> Gratitude is the sign of noble souls.
> - Aesop

I'm thankful of. . . .

I'm thankful of. . . .

I'm thankful of. . . .

Give the image life!

Activities that made me happy today...

1.
2.
3.
4.
5.

My thoughts and ideas today.....

What to do Tomorrow?

1 _______________________________
2 _______________________________
3 _______________________________
4 _______________________________
5 _______________________________

How Do I Feel Today?

Tired

Feelings of Love

Crying

Sleepy

Smiling

Winking

Day 13

Date_____________

> The world gives you way more than you ever
> give it.
> -Kamal Ravikant

I'm thankful of....

I'm thankful of....

I'm thankful of....

Give the image life!

Activities that made me happy today...

1.
2.
3.
4.
5.

My thoughts and ideas today.....

What to do Tomorrow?

1 _______________________________
2 _______________________________
3 _______________________________
4 _______________________________
5 _______________________________

Day 14

Date_____________

> Gratitude is what you feel when you want
> what you already have.
>
> -James Clear

I'm thankful of....

I'm thankful of....

I'm thankful of....

Give the image life!

Activities that made me happy today...

1.
2.
3.
4.
5.

My thoughts and ideas today.....

What to do Tomorrow?

1 ___________________________
2 ___________________________
3 ___________________________
4 ___________________________
5 ___________________________

How Do I Feel Today?

Tired

Feelings of Love

Crying

Sleepy

Smiling

Winking

Date_______________

> No duty is more urgent than that of returning thanks.
> -James Allen

I'm thankful of....

I'm thankful of....

I'm thankful of....

Give the image life!

Activities that made me happy today...

1.
2.
3.
4.
5.

My thoughts and ideas today.....

What to do Tomorrow?

1
2
3
4
5

Tired

Feelings of Love

Crying

Sleepy

Smiling

Winking

<h1 style="text-align:center">Day 16</h1>

Date _______________

I'm thankful of....

I'm thankful of....

I'm thankful of....

Give the image life!

Activities that made me happy today...

1.
2.
3.
4.
5.

My thoughts and ideas today.....

What to do Tomorrow?

1 _______________________
2 _______________________
3 _______________________
4 _______________________
5 _______________________

How Do I Feel Today?

Tired

Feelings of Love

Crying

Sleepy

Smiling

Winking

Date_____________

> Feeling gratitude and not expressing it is
> like wrapping a present and not giving it
> - William Arthur Ward

I'm thankful of....

I'm thankful of....

I'm thankful of....

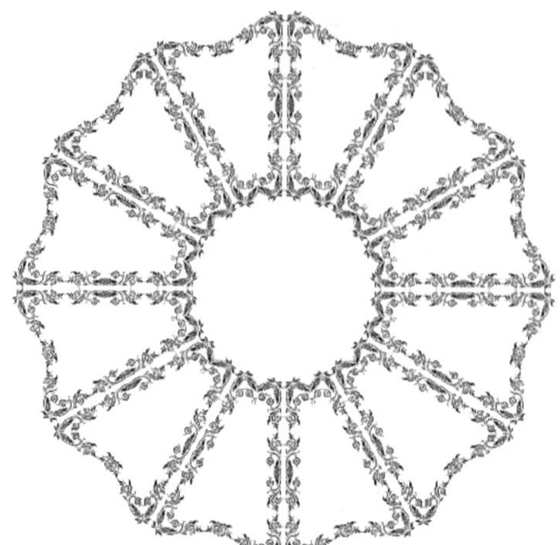

Give the image life!

Activities that made me happy today...

1.
2.
3.
4.
5.

My thoughts and ideas today.....

What to do Tomorrow?

1 _______________________
2 _______________________
3 _______________________
4 _______________________
5 _______________________

How Do I Feel Today?

Tired

Feelings of Love

Crying

Sleepy

Smiling

Winking

Day 18

Date_______________

> When we give cheerfully and accept
> gratefully, everyone is blessed.
> - Maya Angelou

I'm thankful of....

I'm thankful of....

I'm thankful of....

Give the image life!

Activities that made me happy today...

1.
2.
3.
4.
5.

My thoughts and ideas today.....

What to do Tomorrow?

1 _______________________
2 _______________________
3 _______________________
4 _______________________
5 _______________________

How Do I Feel Today?

Tired ☐

Feelings of Love ☐

Crying ☐

Sleepy ☐

Smiling ☐

Winking ☐

Day 19

Date _______________

> As long as this exists, this sunshine and this
> cloudless sky, and as long as I can enjoy
> it, how can I be sad?
> - Anne Frank

I'm thankful of....

I'm thankful of....

I'm thankful of....

Give the image life!

Activities that made me happy today...

1.
2.
3.
4.
5.

My thoughts and ideas today.....

What to do Tomorrow?

1 _______________________
2 _______________________
3 _______________________
4 _______________________
5 _______________________

How Do I Feel Today?

Tired

Feelings of Love

Crying

Sleepy

Smiling

Winking

Date_______________

> In ordinary life, we hardly realize that we
> receive a great deal more than we give, and
> that it is only with gratitude that life
> becomes rich.
> - Dietrich Bonhoeffer

I'm thankful of....

I'm thankful of....

I'm thankful of....

Give the image life!

Activities that made me happy today...

1.
2.
3.
4.
5.

My thoughts and ideas today.....

What to do Tomorrow?

1 _______________________
2 _______________________
3 _______________________
4 _______________________
5 _______________________

Tired

Feelings of Love

Crying

Sleepy

Smiling

Winking

Day 21

Date_______________

Ingratitude is the daughter of pride.
- Miguel de Cervantes

I'm thankful of....

I'm thankful of....

I'm thankful of....

Give the image life!

Activities that made me happy today...

1.
2.
3.
4.
5.

My thoughts and ideas today.....

What to do Tomorrow?

1 _______________________________
2 _______________________________
3 _______________________________
4 _______________________________
5 _______________________________

How Do I Feel Today?

Tired ☐

Feelings of Love ☐

Crying ☐

Sleepy ☐

Smiling ☐

Winking ☐

Day 22

Date______________

> The best way to pay for a lovely moment is
> to enjoy it
> - Richard Bach

I'm thankful of....

I'm thankful of....

I'm thankful of....

Give the image life!

Activities that made me happy today...

1.
2.
3.
4.
5.

My thoughts and ideas today.....

What to do Tomorrow?

1 ___________________________
2 ___________________________
3 ___________________________
4 ___________________________
5 ___________________________

How Do I Feel Today?

Tired ▢

Feelings of Love ▢

Crying ▢

Sleepy ▢

Smiling ▢

Winking ▢

Day 23

Date _____________

> We often take for granted the very things
> that most deserve our gratitude
> — Cynthia Ozick

I'm thankful of....

I'm thankful of....

I'm thankful of....

Give the image life!

Activities that made me happy today...

1.
2.
3.
4.
5.

My thoughts and ideas today.....

What to do Tomorrow?

1. _______________________
2. _______________________
3. _______________________
4. _______________________
5. _______________________

How Do I Feel Today?

Tired

Feelings of Love

Crying

Sleepy

Smiling

Winking

Day 24

Date _______________

> I thank everything, because everything teaches me something.
> - Maxime Lagacé

I'm thankful of....

I'm thankful of....

I'm thankful of....

Give the image life!

Activities that made me happy today...

1.
2.
3.
4.
5.

My thoughts and ideas today.....

What to do Tomorrow?

1 _______________________
2 _______________________
3 _______________________
4 _______________________
5 _______________________

How Do I Feel Today?

Tired

Feelings of Love

Crying

Sleepy

Smiling

Winking

Day 25

Date___________

> Don't pray when it rains if you don't pray
> when the sun shines.
> - Leroy Satchel Paige

I'm thankful of….

I'm thankful of….

I'm thankful of….

Give the image life!

Activities that made me happy today...

1.
2.
3.
4.
5.

My thoughts and ideas today.....

What to do Tomorrow?

1 _______________________________
2 _______________________________
3 _______________________________
4 _______________________________
5 _______________________________

How Do I Feel Today?

Tired

Feelings of Love

Crying

Sleepy

Smiling

Winking

Date________________

We must find time to stop and thank the people
who make a difference in our lives.
- John F. Kennedy

I'm thankful of....

I'm thankful of....

I'm thankful of....

Give the image life!

Activities that made me happy today...

1.
2.
3.
4.
5.

My thoughts and ideas today.....

What to do Tomorrow?

1 ______________________________
2 ______________________________
3 ______________________________
4 ______________________________
5 ______________________________

How Do I Feel Today?

Tired

Feelings of Love

Crying

Sleepy

Smiling

Winking

Day 27

Date _______________

> Meditate, relax and just "be" for a moment.
> Remember that this moment is perfect the way it is
> and you don't need to change it.
> — Maxime Lagacé

I'm thankful of....

I'm thankful of....

I'm thankful of....

Give the image life!

Activities that made me happy today...

1.
2.
3.
4.
5.

My thoughts and ideas today.....

What to do Tomorrow?

1 _______________________
2 _______________________
3 _______________________
4 _______________________
5 _______________________

Day 28

Date________

> Giving thanks for abundance is greater than the abundance itself.
> - Rumi

I'm thankful of….

I'm thankful of….

I'm thankful of….

Give the image life!

Activities that made me happy today...

1.
2.
3.
4.
5.

My thoughts and ideas today.....

What to do Tomorrow?

1 _______________________________
2 _______________________________
3 _______________________________
4 _______________________________
5 _______________________________

How Do I Feel Today?

Tired

Feelings of Love

Crying

Sleepy

Smiling

Winking

Day 29

Date_____________

> A sense of blessedness comes from a change of
> heart, not from more blessings.
>
> — Mason Cooley

I'm thankful of....

I'm thankful of....

I'm thankful of....

Give the image life!

Activities that made me happy today...

1.
2.
3.
4.
5.

My thoughts and ideas today.....

What to do Tomorrow?

1 _______________________
2 _______________________
3 _______________________
4 _______________________
5 _______________________

Day 30

Date_____________

I'm thankful of....

I'm thankful of....

I'm thankful of....

Give the image life!

Activities that made me happy today...

1.
2.
3.
4.
5.

My thoughts and ideas today.....

What to do Tomorrow?

1 _______________________
2 _______________________
3 _______________________
4 _______________________
5 _______________________

How Do I Feel Today?

Tired

Feelings of Love

Crying

Sleepy

Smiling

Winking

Day 31

Date_____________

> When it comes to life the critical thing is whether you take things for granted or take them with gratitude.
> - G.K. Chesterton

I'm thankful of....

I'm thankful of....

I'm thankful of....

Give the image life!

Activities that made me happy today...

1.
2.
3.
4.
5.

My thoughts and ideas today.....

What to do Tomorrow?

1
2
3
4
5

How Do I Feel Today?

Tired

Feelings of Love

Crying

Sleepy

Smiling

Winking

Day 32

Date _____________

We can complain because rose bushes have thorns,
or rejoice because thorns have roses.
- Alphonse Karr

I'm thankful of....

I'm thankful of....

I'm thankful of....

Give the image life!

Activities that made me happy today...

1.
2.
3.
4.
5.

My thoughts and ideas today.....

What to do Tomorrow?

1 ___________________________
2 ___________________________
3 ___________________________
4 ___________________________
5 ___________________________

How Do I Feel Today?

Tired

Feelings of Love

Crying

Sleepy

Smiling

Winking

Date _______________

> I would maintain that thanks are the highest form of thought, and that gratitude is happiness doubled by wonder.
> - Gilbert K. Chesterton

I'm thankful of....

I'm thankful of....

I'm thankful of....

Give the image life!

Activities that made me happy today...

1.
2.
3.
4.
5.

My thoughts and ideas today.....

What to do Tomorrow?

1 _______________________
2 _______________________
3 _______________________
4 _______________________
5 _______________________

How Do I Feel Today?

Tired

Feelings of Love

Crying

Sleepy

Smiling

Winking

Date_____________

> I was complaining that I had no shoes till I met a man who had no feet.
> - Confucius

I'm thankful of....

I'm thankful of....

I'm thankful of....

Give the image life!

Activities that made me happy today...

1.
2.
3.
4.
5.

My thoughts and ideas today.....

What to do Tomorrow?

1______________________________
2______________________________
3______________________________
4______________________________
5______________________________

How Do I Feel Today?

Tired

Feelings of Love

Crying

Sleepy

Smiling

Winking

Day 35

Date_____________

Gratitude is the memory of the heart.
- Jean Baptiste Massieu

I'm thankful of....

I'm thankful of....

I'm thankful of....

Give the image life!

Activities that made me happy today. . .

1.
2.
3.
4.
5.

My thoughts and ideas today. . . . .

What to do Tomorrow?

1 _______________________________
2 _______________________________
3 _______________________________
4 _______________________________
5 _______________________________

How Do I Feel Today?

Tired

Feelings of Love

Crying

Sleepy

Smiling

Winking

Day 36

Date _____________

> Gratitude is a quality similar to electricity: it must be produced and discharged and used up in order to exist at all.
> — William Faulkner

I'm thankful of....

I'm thankful of....

I'm thankful of....

Give the image life!

Activities that made me happy today...

1.
2.
3.
4.
5.

My thoughts and ideas today.....

What to do Tomorrow?

1 ___________________________
2 ___________________________
3 ___________________________
4 ___________________________
5 ___________________________

How Do I Feel Today?

Tired

Feelings of Love

Crying

Sleepy

Smiling

Winking

Day 37

Date________________

> Gratitude is an opener of locked up blessings
> - Marianne Williamson

I'm thankful of....

I'm thankful of....

I'm thankful of....

Give the image life!

Activities that made me happy today...

1.
2.
3.
4.
5.

My thoughts and ideas today.....

What to do Tomorrow?

1 ___________________________
2 ___________________________
3 ___________________________
4 ___________________________
5 ___________________________

How Do I Feel Today?

Tired

Feelings of Love

Crying

Sleepy

Smiling

Winking

Day 38

Date ___________

> Gratitude is merely the secret hope of further favors.
> - François de La Rochefoucauld

I'm thankful of....

I'm thankful of....

I'm thankful of....

Give the image life!

Activities that made me happy today...

1.
2.
3.
4.
5.

My thoughts and ideas today.....

What to do Tomorrow?

1 ___________________________
2 ___________________________
3 ___________________________
4 ___________________________
5 ___________________________

Tired

Feelings of Love

Crying

Sleepy

Smiling

Winking

Day 39

Date _______________

> Gratitude is the least of the virtues, but ingratitude is the worst of vices.
>
> — Thomas Fuller

I'm thankful of....

I'm thankful of....

I'm thankful of....

Give the image life!

Activities that made me happy today...

1.
2.
3.
4.
5.

My thoughts and ideas today.....

What to do Tomorrow?

1 _______________________________
2 _______________________________
3 _______________________________
4 _______________________________
5 _______________________________

How Do I Feel Today?

Tired ☐

Feelings of Love ☐

Crying ☐

Sleepy ☐

Smiling ☐

Winking ☐

Day 40

Date____________

> Gratitude is a currency that we can mint for ourselves, and spend without fear of bankruptcy.
> - Fred De Witt Van Amburgh

I'm thankful of....

I'm thankful of....

I'm thankful of....

Activities that made me happy today...

1.
2.
3.
4.
5.

My thoughts and ideas today.....

What to do Tomorrow?

1 _______________________
2 _______________________
3 _______________________
4 _______________________
5 _______________________

Date __________

Day 41

> Gratitude is the ability to experience life as a gift. It liberates us from the prison of self preoccupation.
> - John Ortberg

I'm thankful of....

I'm thankful of....

I'm thankful of....

Give the image life!

Activities that made me happy today...

1.
2.
3.
4.
5.

My thoughts and ideas today.....

What to do Tomorrow?

1_______________________
2_______________________
3_______________________
4_______________________
5_______________________

How Do I Feel Today?

Tired

Feelings of Love

Crying

Sleepy

Smiling

Winking

Day 42

Date_____________

> Forget injuries, never forget kindnesses.
> - Confucius

I'm thankful of....

I'm thankful of....

I'm thankful of....

Give the image life!

Activities that made me happy today...

```
1.
2.
3.
4.
5.
```

My thoughts and ideas today.....

What to do Tomorrow?

```
1 ___________________________
2 ___________________________
3 ___________________________
4 ___________________________
5 ___________________________
```

Day 43

Date _______________

> Gratitude is not only the greatest of virtues but the parent of all others. Marcus Tellius
> - Cicero

I'm thankful of....

I'm thankful of....

I'm thankful of....

Give the image life!

Activities that made me happy today...

1.
2.
3.
4.
5.

My thoughts and ideas today.....

What to do Tomorrow?

1 _______________________
2 _______________________
3 _______________________
4 _______________________
5 _______________________

How Do I Feel Today?

Tired

Feelings of Love

Crying

Sleepy

Smiling

Winking

Day 44

Date _______________

> The smallest act of kindness is worth than the grandest intention.
>
> — Oscar Wilde

I'm thankful of....

I'm thankful of....

I'm thankful of....

Give the image life!

Activities that made me happy today...

1.
2.
3.
4.
5.

My thoughts and ideas today.....

What to do Tomorrow?

1 _______________________
2 _______________________
3 _______________________
4 _______________________
5 _______________________

How Do I Feel Today?

Tired

Feelings of Love

Crying

Sleepy

Smiling

Winking

Day 45

Date _____________

> *The essence of all beautiful art is gratitude.* -
> Friedrich Nietzsche

I'm thankful of....

I'm thankful of....

I'm thankful of....

Give the image life!

Activities that made me happy today...

1.
2.
3.
4.
5.

My thoughts and ideas today.....

What to do Tomorrow?

1 _______________________________
2 _______________________________
3 _______________________________
4 _______________________________
5 _______________________________

How Do I Feel Today?

Tired

Feelings of Love

Crying

Sleepy

Smiling

Winking

Day 46

Date______________

> Gratitude is a duty which ought to be paid, but which none have a right to expect.
> - Jean-Jacques Rousseau

I'm thankful of….

I'm thankful of….

I'm thankful of….

Give the image life!

Activities that made me happy today...

1.
2.
3.
4.
5.

My thoughts and ideas today.....

What to do Tomorrow?

1______________________________
2______________________________
3______________________________
4______________________________
5______________________________

How Do I Feel Today?

Tired

Feelings of Love

Crying

Sleepy

Smiling

Winking

Day 47

Date ______________

> He is a wise man who does not grieve for the things
> which he has not, but rejoices for those which he has.
> - Epictetus

I'm thankful of....

I'm thankful of....

I'm thankful of....

Give the image life!

Activities that made me happy today...

1.
2.
3.
4.
5.

My thoughts and ideas today.....

What to do Tomorrow?

1_______________________
2_______________________
3_______________________
4_______________________
5_______________________

Tired

Feelings of Love

Crying

Sleepy

Smiling

Winking

Date_______________

> The deepest craving of human nature is the need to
> be appreciated
> - William James

I'm thankful of....

I'm thankful of....

I'm thankful of....

Give the image life!

Activities that made me happy today...

1.
2.
3.
4.
5.

My thoughts and ideas today.....

What to do Tomorrow?

1 _______________________
2 _______________________
3 _______________________
4 _______________________
5 _______________________

How Do I Feel Today?

Tired

Feelings of Love

Crying

Sleepy

Smiling

Winking

Day 49

Date _______________

> *Our favorite attitude should be gratitude.*
> — Zig Ziglar

I'm thankful of….

I'm thankful of….

I'm thankful of….

Give the image life!

Activities that made me happy today...

1.
2.
3.
4.
5.

My thoughts and ideas today.....

What to do Tomorrow?

1 _______________________________
2 _______________________________
3 _______________________________
4 _______________________________
5 _______________________________

How Do I Feel Today?

Tired ☐

Feelings of Love ☐

Crying ☐

Sleepy ☐

Smiling ☐

Winking ☐

Day 50

Date _______________

True forgiveness is when you can say, "Thank you for that experience".

\- Oprah Winfrey

I'm thankful of....

I'm thankful of....

I'm thankful of....

Give the image life!

Activities that made me happy today...

1.
2.
3.
4.
5.

My thoughts and ideas today.....

What to do Tomorrow?

1 _______________________________
2 _______________________________
3 _______________________________
4 _______________________________
5 _______________________________

Tired

Feelings of Love

Crying

Sleepy

Smiling

Winking

Day 51

Date _____________

> *Ingratitude is monstrous.*
> - William Shakespeare

I'm thankful of....

I'm thankful of....

I'm thankful of....

Give the image life!

Activities that made me happy today...

1.
2.
3.
4.
5.

My thoughts and ideas today.....

What to do Tomorrow?

1________________________
2________________________
3________________________
4________________________
5________________________

How Do I Feel Today?

Tired

Feelings of Love

Crying

Sleepy

Smiling

Winking

Day 52

Date____________

> Nothing is more honorable than a grateful heart.
> - Seneca

I'm thankful of….

I'm thankful of….

I'm thankful of….

Give the image life!

Activities that made me happy today...

1.
2.
3.
4.
5.

My thoughts and ideas today......

What to do Tomorrow?

1 _______________________
2 _______________________
3 _______________________
4 _______________________
5 _______________________

How Do I Feel Today?

Tired

Feelings of Love

Crying

Sleepy

Smiling

Winking

Day 53

Date___________

> *Act with kindness, but do not expect gratitude.*
> — Confucius

I'm thankful of....

I'm thankful of....

I'm thankful of....

Give the image life!

Activities that made me happy today...

1.
2.
3.
4.
5.

My thoughts and ideas today.....

What to do Tomorrow?

1 _______________________
2 _______________________
3 _______________________
4 _______________________
5 _______________________

How Do I Feel Today?

Tired ☐

Feelings of Love ☐

Crying ☐

Sleepy ☐

Smiling ☐

Winking ☐

Day 54

Date _______________

I'm thankful of....

I'm thankful of....

I'm thankful of....

Give the image life!

Activities that made me happy today...

1.
2.
3.
4.
5.

My thoughts and ideas today.....

What to do Tomorrow?

1 _______________________
2 _______________________
3 _______________________
4 _______________________
5 _______________________

Tired

Feelings of Love

Crying

Sleepy

Smiling

Winking

Day 55

Date________________

I'm thankful of....

I'm thankful of....

I'm thankful of....

Give the image life!

Activities that made me happy today...

> 1.
> 2.
> 3.
> 4.
> 5.

My thoughts and ideas today.....

What to do Tomorrow?

1 _______________________________
2 _______________________________
3 _______________________________
4 _______________________________
5 _______________________________

Day 56

Date____________

> Entitlement is such a cancer, because it is void of gratitude.
>
> — Adam Smith

I'm thankful of....

I'm thankful of....

I'm thankful of....

Give the image life!

Activities that made me happy today...

1.
2.
3.
4.
5.

My thoughts and ideas today.....

What to do Tomorrow?

1
2
3
4
5

How Do I Feel Today?

Tired

Feelings of Love

Crying

Sleepy

Smiling

Winking

Day 57

Date_____________

> There are always flowers for those who want to see them.
> - Henri Matisse

I'm thankful of....

I'm thankful of....

I'm thankful of....

Give the image life!

Activities that made me happy today...

1.
2.
3.
4.
5.

My thoughts and ideas today.....

What to do Tomorrow?

1 ___________________________
2 ___________________________
3 ___________________________
4 ___________________________
5 ___________________________

How Do I Feel Today?

Tired

Feelings of Love

Crying

Sleepy

Smiling

Winking

Day 58

Date_____________

Giving is an expression of gratitude for our blessings.
- Laura Arrillaga-Andreessen

I'm thankful of....

I'm thankful of....

I'm thankful of....

Give the image life!

Activities that made me happy today...

1.
2.
3.
4.
5.

My thoughts and ideas today.....

What to do Tomorrow?

1_______________________
2_______________________
3_______________________
4_______________________
5_______________________

How Do I Feel Today?

Tired

Feelings of Love

Crying

Sleepy

Smiling

Winking

Day 59

Date _____________

I'm thankful of....

I'm thankful of....

I'm thankful of....

Give the image life!

Activities that made me happy today...

1.
2.
3.
4.
5.

My thoughts and ideas today......

What to do Tomorrow?

1 _______________________
2 _______________________
3 _______________________
4 _______________________
5 _______________________

Tired

Feelings of Love

Crying

Sleepy

Smiling

Winking

Day 60

Date _____________

> Hope has a good memory, gratitude a bad one.
> - Baltasar Gracian

I'm thankful of....

I'm thankful of....

I'm thankful of....

Give the image life!

Activities that made me happy today...

1.
2.
3.
4.
5.

My thoughts and ideas today.....

What to do Tomorrow?

1_______________________
2_______________________
3_______________________
4_______________________
5_______________________

How Do I Feel Today?

Tired

Feelings of Love

Crying

Sleepy

Smiling

Winking

Day 61

Date _____________

> *Every blessing ignored becomes a curse.*
> — Paulo Coelho

I'm thankful of....

I'm thankful of....

I'm thankful of....

Give the image life!

Activities that made me happy today. . .

1.
2.
3.
4.
5.

My thoughts and ideas today. . . . .

What to do Tomorrow?

1 _______________________________
2 _______________________________
3 _______________________________
4 _______________________________
5 _______________________________

How Do I Feel Today?

Tired

Feelings of Love

Crying

Sleepy

Smiling

Winking

Day 62

Date_____________

Find the good and praise it.
 - Alex Haley

I'm thankful of....

I'm thankful of....

I'm thankful of....

Give the image life!

Activities that made me happy today...

1.
2.
3.
4.
5.

My thoughts and ideas today.....

What to do Tomorrow?

1______________________________
2______________________________
3______________________________
4______________________________
5______________________________

How Do I Feel Today?

Tired

Feelings of Love

Crying

Sleepy

Smiling

Winking

Day 63

Date _______________

> *Things must be felt with the heart.*
> — Helen Keller

I'm thankful of. . . .

I'm thankful of. . . .

I'm thankful of. . . .

Give the image life!

Activities that made me happy today...

1.
2.
3.
4.
5.

My thoughts and ideas today.....

What to do Tomorrow?

1 __________________________
2 __________________________
3 __________________________
4 __________________________
5 __________________________

Tired

Feelings of Love

Crying

Sleepy

Smiling

Winking

Day 64

Date________________

I'm thankful of….

I'm thankful of….

I'm thankful of….

Give the image life!

Activities that made me happy today...

1.
2.
3.
4.
5.

My thoughts and ideas today.....

What to do Tomorrow?

1_______________________
2_______________________
3_______________________
4_______________________
5_______________________

How Do I Feel Today?

Tired

Feelings of Love

Crying

Sleepy

Smiling

Winking

Day 65

Date _______________

> No blessing lasts forever.
>
> — Plautus

I'm thankful of....

I'm thankful of....

I'm thankful of....

Give the image life!

Activities that made me happy today...

1.
2.
3.
4.
5.

My thoughts and ideas today.....

What to do Tomorrow?

1 _______________________
2 _______________________
3 _______________________
4 _______________________
5 _______________________

How Do I Feel Today?

Tired

Feelings of Love

Crying

Sleepy

Smiling

Winking

Day 66

Date___________

> *Appreciation is the purest vibration that exists on the planet today.*
>
> - Abraham Hicks

I'm thankful of....

I'm thankful of....

I'm thankful of....

Give the image life!

Activities that made me happy today...

1.
2.
3.
4.
5.

My thoughts and ideas today.....

What to do Tomorrow?

1_______________________________
2_______________________________
3_______________________________
4_______________________________
5_______________________________

How Do I Feel Today?

Tired

Feelings of Love

Crying

Sleepy

Smiling

Winking

Day 67

Date________________

If you have lived, take thankfully the past.

— John Dryden

I'm thankful of....

I'm thankful of....

I'm thankful of....

Give the image life!

Activities that made me happy today...

1.
2.
3.
4.
5.

My thoughts and ideas today.....

What to do Tomorrow?

1 _______________________________
2 _______________________________
3 _______________________________
4 _______________________________
5 _______________________________

How Do I Feel Today?

Tired

Feelings of Love

Crying

Sleepy

Smiling

Winking

Day 68

Date___________

> If you are really thankful, what do you do? You share.
>
> — W. Clement Stone

I'm thankful of....

I'm thankful of....

I'm thankful of....

Give the image life!

Activities that made me happy today...

1.
2.
3.
4.
5.

My thoughts and ideas today.....

What to do Tomorrow?

1 _______________________________
2 _______________________________
3 _______________________________
4 _______________________________
5 _______________________________

How Do I Feel Today?

Tired ☐

Feelings of Love ☐

Crying ☐

Sleepy ☐

Smiling ☐

Winking ☐

Day 69

Date _____________

> Ingratitude is treason to mankind.
> — James Thomson

I'm thankful of....

I'm thankful of....

I'm thankful of....

Give the image life!

Activities that made me happy today...

1.
2.
3.
4.
5.

My thoughts and ideas today.....

What to do Tomorrow?

1 _______________________________
2 _______________________________
3 _______________________________
4 _______________________________
5 _______________________________

Day 70

Date __________

May the gratitude in my heart kiss all the universe.
- Hafiz

I'm thankful of....

I'm thankful of....

I'm thankful of....

Give the image life!

Activities that made me happy today...

1.
2.
3.
4.
5.

My thoughts and ideas today.....

What to do Tomorrow?

1_______________________________
2_______________________________
3_______________________________
4_______________________________
5_______________________________

How Do I Feel Today?

Tired

Feelings of Love

Crying

Sleepy

Smiling

Winking

Day 71

Date _______________

> Gratitude unlocks the fullness of life.
> — Melody Beattie

I'm thankful of....

I'm thankful of....

I'm thankful of....

Give the image life!

Activities that made me happy today...

1.
2.
3.
4.
5.

My thoughts and ideas today.....

What to do Tomorrow?

1 _______________________________
2 _______________________________
3 _______________________________
4 _______________________________
5 _______________________________

Tired

Feelings of Love

Crying

Sleepy

Smiling

Winking

Day 72

Date _____________

> The highest tribute to the dead is not grief but gratitude.
> — Thornton Wilder

I'm thankful of....

I'm thankful of....

I'm thankful of....

Give the image life!

Activities that made me happy today...

1.
2.
3.
4.
5.

My thoughts and ideas today.....

What to do Tomorrow?

1 _______________________
2 _______________________
3 _______________________
4 _______________________
5 _______________________

Tired

Feelings of Love

Crying

Sleepy

Smiling

Winking

Day 73

Date ___________

> Three meals plus bedtime make four sure blessings a day.
>
> — Mason Cooley

I'm thankful of….

I'm thankful of….

I'm thankful of….

Give the image life!

Activities that made me happy today...

1.
2.
3.
4.
5.

My thoughts and ideas today.....

What to do Tomorrow?

1 _______________________________
2 _______________________________
3 _______________________________
4 _______________________________
5 _______________________________

How Do I Feel Today?

Tired ☐

Feelings of Love ☐

Crying ☐

Sleepy ☐

Smiling ☐

Winking ☐

Day 74

Date _______________

> *Gratitude and attitude are not challenges; they are choices.*
> - Robert Braathe

I'm thankful of....

I'm thankful of....

I'm thankful of....

Give the image life!

Activities that made me happy today...

1.
2.
3.
4.
5.

My thoughts and ideas today.....

What to do Tomorrow?

1_______________________________
2_______________________________
3_______________________________
4_______________________________
5_______________________________

Tired

Feelings of Love

Crying

Sleepy

Smiling

Winking

Day 75

Date __________

> *Appreciation is a wonderful thing. It makes what is excellent in others belong to us as well*
>
> — Voltaire

I'm thankful of....

I'm thankful of....

I'm thankful of....

Give the image life!

Activities that made me happy today...

1.
2.
3.
4.
5.

My thoughts and ideas today.....

What to do Tomorrow?

1 _______________________________
2 _______________________________
3 _______________________________
4 _______________________________
5 _______________________________

How Do I Feel Today?

Tired

Feelings of Love

Crying

Sleepy

Smiling

Winking

www.ingramcontent.com/pod-product-compliance
Lightning Source LLC
Chambersburg PA
CBHW071436130726
47997CB00006B/2113